AF327387

Women's March on Idaho
January 21st, 2017

BANNOCK
WE WILL
WOMEN'S PLACE IS IN THE REVOLUTION
RAPE CULTURE
THIS IS MY
I don't know her
I don't Know
OUR BODIES OUR MINDS OUR POWER!
SPEAK UP SPEAK OUT
WOMEN
We the PEOPLE
WOMEN
TRY REACHING UP MY PUSSY!!!
THE RACI UNST MISO PLUT
WE ARE JUST GETTING
Freedom of Speech
FIGHTING FOR MY SON
PEACE LOVE LENCE
WITHOUT FEAR WITHOUT

I MARCH FOR MY DAUGHTER
WHAT SHE SAID
BIGOTRY IS NOT PATRIOTISM
Equality FOR ALL
MEANS
Dump Trump Bring Back Barack
I STAND WITH PLANNED PARENTHOOD
DEFEND EQUALITY
DON'T
RIGHTS!!!
BANNOCK

HEALTH CARE IS
A HUMAN RIGHT
We

PLANNED PARENTHOOD
Saves LIVES

I STAN
WITH
PLANNE
PARENT
Planned Parenthood
AND
TH
ANNED
ARENTHOOD
anned Parenthood
LOVE

We Cannot Succeed
ALL men can
understand =
A A DRESS is
NOT A YES

THIS
GIRL
CAN!
If he builds a
Wall. I'll grow
up and tear it
DOWN!

If he builds a
Wall. I'll grow
up and tear it
DOWN!
WOMENS
RIGHTS
ARE
HUMAN
RIGHTS

TREAT
OTHERS
FAIRLY

I STAND WITH PLANNED PARENTHOOD
Planned Parenthood
Why I March
Women's Rights
Equality =
Peace
Liberty
Justice
I STAND WITH PLANNED PARENTHOOD
I STAND WITH PLANNED PARENTHOOD
Keep your tiny hands OFF
Just "FIGHT" to 22422 STAND WITH
NO GRAB

UNITED 4 ALL
WOMEN
WCW
EQUAL
Empowered Women
Dump Trump Bring Back Barack
Show us the Tax Returns
I'M A NASTY WOMAN THAT VOTES
HATE
WITHOUT FEAR WITHOUT APOLOGY
I CAN'T
WILL NOT
HATE
WHY I MARCH
RACISM
NOT WOMEN NOT
NOT ALL

NOT
AFRAID
OF
BULLIES

#pawsoffpussies

THE
FUTURE
IS
NASTY

Make America KIND again
HATE

Girls just wanna have Fundamental Human Rights
I'm with HER
YOU LOVE
READ

I'M A NASTY
WOMAN
THAT VOTES

RUDENESS IS
THE WEAK PERSONS
IMITATION OF
STRENGTH

LORD
JAN 21 AT 10 AM 2:45 & 7:30 PM
Don't Take Away Our Care
STAND WITH PLANNED PARENTHOOD
BLACK LIVES MATTER
PLANNED PARENTHOOD
EQUALITY
CHILDREN'S RIGHTS
LOVE PEACE HUMAN DIGNI
because

Love
not hate
makes
America Great
AVAILABLE
208.794.8020

I STAND WITH PLANNED PARENTHOOD
I STAND
ND
THOOD
AND
ED

THOMAS HAMMER
LOVE WILL TRIUMPH
One World
FREE CONTRACEPTION PREVENTS ABORTIONS
I stand with PLANNED PARENTHOOD!

THE FUTURE IS NASTY
I'M with HER↓
YOU DON'T NEED SUPER POWERS TO BE A HERO
NOT AFRAID OF BULLIES
PRINCESS DIVA CAPABLE SWEETIE DOLL GIRL

BEWARE!
IDAHO IS FULL
OF NASTY WOMEN

I WILL NOT
GO QUIETLY
BACK TO THE
FIFTIES!

respect
existence
—OR—
expect
resistance

We need to TALK
about the
ELEPHANT
in the womb
with LIBERTY
and JUSTICE
for A

THIS IS
VERY
BAD!
Still...
NOT
my
President

I am a Christian
Climate Change
Planned Parenthood
WHY I
MARCH
PRISON REFORM
EQUALITY FOR ALL
PEOPLE
RACISM
NAMASTE

PUSSY
POWER
#WOMENSMARCH

DEFEND EQUALITY LOVE UNITES
WOMEN'S MARCH
IDAHO
Text MARCH to 77948

We cannot
succeed when
HALF of us are
HELD BACK
SHATTER
that
glass
CEILING

Equal
PAY
for Equal
WE THE PEOPLE
ARE GREATER THAN FEAR
NEV
GIV

WOMEN ARE PERF

PUSSY
GRABS
BACK

These Violent
Delights Have
Violent Ends

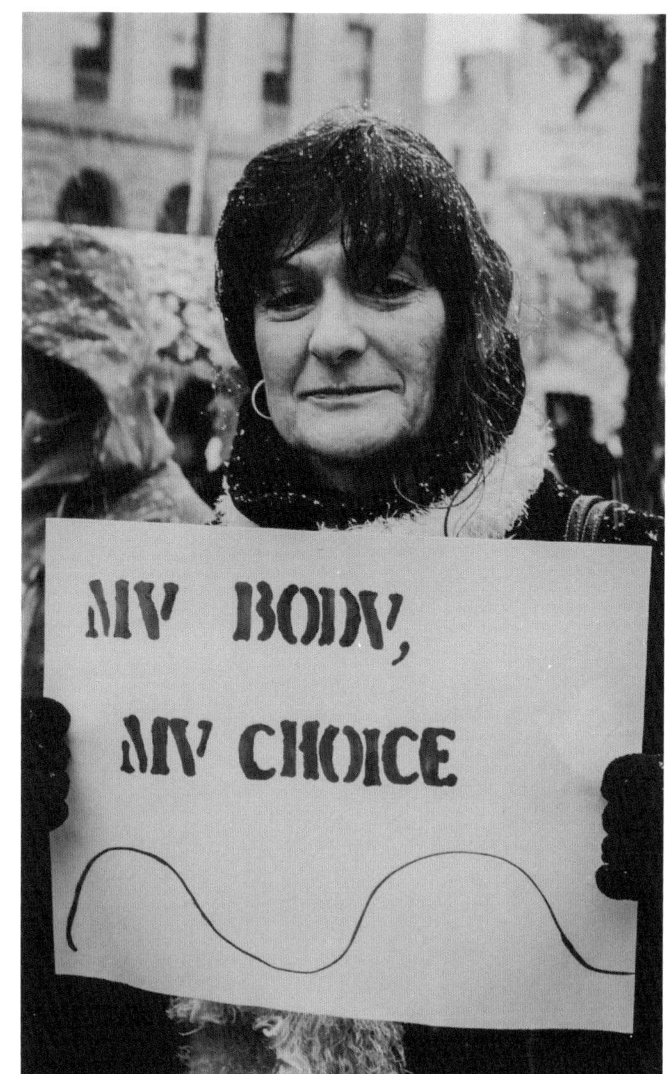
MY BODY,
MY CHOICE

MEN OF
QUALITY
DON'T FEAR
EQUALITY
PROUD
OWNER OF A
VAGINA

A
Woman's
Place
Is In
The
Resistance
Rebellions
are built on
HOPE

RESERVED
PARKING
IDAHO STATE
POLICE
OUR
RIGHTS
AREN'T
UP FOR
GRABS

STAND
Why I March
Women's Rights
OD
FIGHT
to
22422
STAND WITH
WO
MA
-ID
Text M

All of
Defend DIGNITY
WE THE PEOPLE
MEN'S
RCH
AHO —
RCH to 77948

Dear Idahoans,

This is a message from Colette Raptosh and Nora Harrren. Last year it was an absolute honor to be able to give back and march along side you guys on January 21st 2017. You would never believe our faces when we looked out from the top of the Idaho State Capitol steps and saw pools of pink pussy hats and umbrellas coming from every direction. It was a sight for sore eyes to see 7,000 Idahoans marching in the snow for women's rights and it filled our hearts with pride and power. As a community, we have never been more unified and we must always make a conscious effort to stick together. Without knowing what was to come, on November 12th 2016 at the very first rally we ever organized together, we said:

"I have faith in this city, the people around me, and the people here today. That we have it in us to look past our own gender, skin color, religion, and sexuality. That if we can come together and stand strong without turning our back on someone, our community can grow and become stronger as a whole, and with that, be able to endure anything the country may go through." -Colette Raptosh

"I want to leave you with this...diversity is an integral component of the United States, it is crucial that we can disagree without being disagreeable. We are strong alone, but we are stronger together." -Nora Harren

Describing the feeling we had on the historic day would be nearly impossible, but we can try. It felt like years of silence was turned in power and in our hearts it felt like the world had changed. Maybe not a huge change, but like Idaho would never be quite the same. We can't believe it has been a whole year since the march and it feels like just yesterday we were skipping school for meetings and getting our phones taken away in class for emailing our speakers. Look how far we have come. We took the first steps in a long march and since then, we have had the school education rally, the scientist's rally, the Daca rally, huddles, and so much more. Along with our victories, we all know it is a marathon, not a sprint, but we will be with you every step of the way.

Xoxo,
Colette Raptosh
& Nora Harren

Contributing Photographers:
Andy McCutcheon
Sam Sandmire
Ellen Hansen
AAUW Boise
Kimberly Weathers
Lindsey Stanton
Cristina Lee Patterson
Tanya Gordon
Leah DeSantis
Colton Rothwell
Lori Fascilla
Emily Allen
Fiona Montagne
Book Designed and Cover Art by Colton Rothwell

CPSIA information can be obtained at www.ICGtesting.com
Printed in the USA
LVIW01n1016090118
562325LV00001B/5